Liberated

Freed From the Flagpole

The Metamorphosis of the Flag Since 9/11

Robert Carley's Photo Journey & Journal

WestBow Press books may be ordered through booksellers or by contacting:

WestBow Press
A Division of Thomas Nelson & Zondervan
1663 Liberty Drive
Bloomington, IN 47403
www.westbowpress.com
844-714-3454

Author Photo by Noroton Media

Scripture taken from the King James Version of the Bible.

ISBN: 978-1-6642-3387-4 (sc)
ISBN: 978-1-6642-3389-8 (hc)
ISBN: 978-1-6642-3388-1 (e)

Library of Congress Control Number: 2021909211

Print information available on the last page.

WestBow Press rev. date: 08/12/2021

WESTBOW
PRESS®
A DIVISION OF THOMAS NELSON
& ZONDERVAN

This book is dedicated to the 2,997 individuals who perished on Tuesday, September 11, 2001, and in honor of the 3,051 children who lost a parent on that tragic day.

Observation Deck, Plywood Platform Overlooking the Pit at Ground Zero, 2002

In 2011, this photo was used for *New York Magazine's* online 10-year anniversary feature, "Encyclopedia of 9/11."

ACKNOWLEDGMENTS

Special thanks to my wife, Joy, who gave me valuable advice in the preparation of this book and who endured a 3,000 mile photography trip without getting car sick. I want to thank my good hometown buddies: Paul, Charles, Barrett, and Marc. Thanks to everyone along the way that I stopped to ask for directions and leads. Thanks to all the police officers, mail carriers and firefighters who gave me tips to finding flag displays all over the country, including Tracy of the Grandview, Missouri, police department. She put out a calling-all-cars dispatch for all police officers to help me locate the address of a specific flag house in the town! Thanks to my father Robert G. Carley, who after he died in 1993, left me his old 1979 Nikon FA, which inspired me to take up photography in the spring of 2001. Thanks to my mother Eliane Ame-Leroy Carley, who helped to financially support my many road trips. I have been working on publishing a 9/11 photo book for many years. Back in 2002 or 2003, I was working on it at the computer lab of Norwalk Community College. I was walking down a hallway there holding a white 10-inch-by-12-inch box of notes and printouts of my first flag book attempt. The governor of Connecticut at the time, John G. Rowland, surrounded by a large crowd, was visiting the campus, and as we walked by each other in the hallway he smiled at me and joked, "What do you have there? A cake?" About 18 years later, I never thought that the governor would be associated with my book. I appreciate Governor Rowland for writing a blurb for *Liberated: Freed From the Flagpole*. A "Godwink!" Lastly, I would like to acknowledge Jeffrey Brunson, former Iraq War veteran and now LED face mask entrepreneur, whom I met at a rest stop. His photos are the last ones to be included in the book.

A boxing club sign located near Ground Zero.

PHOTOGRAPHER

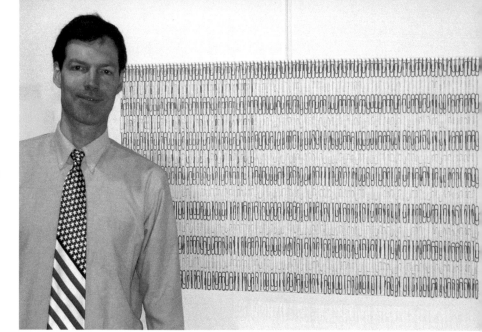

Noroton Media Photo, 2008

Robert Carley was born in New Orleans, Louisiana. His mother was the daughter of a French ambassador and his father was president of a large advertising agency based in New Orleans. His great uncle, Maxime Leroy, was a great historian and an elite member of the Académie Française.

He graduated from the University of Pennsylvania, where he received a BA, double majoring in political science and fine arts. Over the past 20 years, Carley has had the opportunity, mostly due to layoffs — first as a result of 9/11 and again thanks to the financial crisis of 2009 — to take multiple flag photo, cross-country road trips. To help support his photography financially, he became a SAG background actor working on many hit TV shows, such as "Blue Bloods," "Law and Order," "Person of Interest" and "Elementary." He has also worked on movies and was featured in several, including the Academy Award-winning movie *Still Alice.*

Carley's photographs have been featured on the websites of the BBC, Microsoft News, National Journal, *Baltimore Sun, The Washington Times, Hartford Courant, San Francisco Chronicle, New York Magazine* and *Connecticut Magazine.* He has had solo shows of his flag photos at the Star-Spangled Banner Flag House Museum in Baltimore, the Museum of Connecticut History in Hartford, the Connecticut State Capitol, and for the 20th anniversary of 9/11 at the Mattatuck Museum in Waterbury, Connecticut. The 9/11 Memorial & Museum selected 165 of his photographs for their permanent collection.

Carley was so inspired by taking photos of other people's flag tributes that he started making his own. These flags were fashioned out of coffee-cup lids, creamer containers, water bottles, automobile tires, shuttle cocks, tape cassettes, VHS tapes and egg cartons. His paper clip flag (above) was chosen for an exhibit by well-known sculptor James Grashow. Many of these creations were featured on news broadcasts in New York City, Hartford, Connecticut, and in Fairfield County, Connecticut.

Carley's other artistic pursuits include caricature and abstract art. A caricature of George H.W. Bush was exhibited in a show titled "To the President: Folk Portraits by the People" at the Smithsonian's National Portrait Gallery in 1994. One of his abstract drawings was awarded Best in Show at the Greenwich Art Society by a curator from the Metropolitan Museum of Art.

INTRODUCTION

Packed for my red, white, and blue road trips with essentials — sunglasses, tire pressure gauge, and camera.

Looking out from my office window towards the skyline of New York City on September the 11, 2001, I watched history unfold before my very eyes. The sight of the billowing smoke from the Twin Towers will forever be etched in my memory. But as soon as the Ground Zero ashes had cooled off and the dark clouds of disbelief lifted, a red-hot patriotism started spreading like a wildfire across the country. Nothing could douse it. This fire touched every corner of the country, from remote small-town America to the large urban centers. Americans felt the desire to show their love, compassion and goodwill to their fellow citizens. The flag was the symbol they used to show each other that they could persevere and overcome.

Putting down my artist's pen in favor of the camera, I began in earnest a 20-year documentary journey to capture this American spirit. I started off snapping photos in my neighborhood, my town, then all across my state, then finally branching out to all regions of the U.S. Traveling alone, I crisscrossed 45 states in my hunt to discover as many flag tributes as possible. I enjoyed every minute of it — eating at local diners, talking to friendly locals and always finding things that I never expected. I felt an urgency, knowing that a lot of the displays would have a short life span, I wanted to preserve the images for historical purposes. The few years after 9/11 especially represented a unique time in American history.

Americans over the past twenty years have been breaking tradition and respectfully taking liberties with "Old Glory." The flag is no longer only a piece of fabric attached to a flagpole; it has been freed and untethered. The major reason? After 9/11, they flew off the shelves and sold out. American ingenuity came to the fore. Citizens have transformed the flag to express their patriotic zeal, using personal materials or objects they had on hand. With great imagination and creativity, the flag continues to evolve. The wide range of unconventional materials used are surprising and sometimes amusing: flag-painted cars, trees, murals, houses, and even flag-tattooed people.

After all these years, I am still finding wonderful flag images and writing the stories behind them. Every time I start off on a road trip, I begin with a short prayer: "God help me to find beautiful flags today." More often than not, I am surprised that God actually answered my prayer, and helped me be at the right place and at the right time. To this day, I am excited to see what He has in store for me. "In all your ways acknowledge Him, And He shall direct your paths," (Proverbs 3:6, NKJV). Some of my amazing "Godincidences," or "Godwinks," are recounted in the following pages.

Robert Carley, Darien, Connecticut

Liberated

Freed From the Flagpole

Robert Carley's Photo Journey & Journal

Patriotism Branching Out
Newtown, Connecticut 2002

An artist named David spent 70 hours painting these maple trees, a project commissioned by Howard, a Wall Street executive who had lost nine friends on 9/11. This was his way of creating a "living" memorial in honor of his colleagues.

Bethie's Stick/Saplings Flag, America Sticking Together!
Adirondack Mountains, Chestertown, New York 2002

I spotted this fading flag leaning against an old garage on an isolated stretch of a backwoods country road. Bethie, a former teacher, her young son Creedence, and her nephew Johnny worked on it together for two days. It was placed there after 9/11 and was colored by using dyes taken from the flowers and roots gathered from the area woods.

The top photo was part of a slide show of my photos posted on the BBC website to remember the 10th anniversary of 9/11.

Home Front
Kent, Connecticut 2002

Kevin started painting his house like a flag one week after 9/11. He received this inspiration from a dream. About 14 miles up the road in the town of Sharon lives the great artist Jasper Johns, who painted the iconic encaustic "Flag" (1954–55). Coincidently, both men had dreams about painting flags. Always a patriotic person, Kevin told me, "When my son was growing up, I used to tell him that we had red, white, and blue blood."

One 23-year-old Kent resident lost his life on 9/11.

The key to Kevin's front door.

1966 V8 Pontiac Bonneville
Darien, Connecticut 2002

I stumbled upon this muscle car the same day I was anxiously trying to reach someone else who had painted their car like a flag. The owner also had a flag tattooed on his back. Mark told me "The car is a rolling reminder of lives lost and heroes born before, on, and after that tragic day in September." "It was the day after my car became a canvas for our flag."

The biggest reaction Mark has had to date was when a group of young women serenaded him with the "Star-Spangled Banner." After all these years Mark still has the car, which is stored in his barn. American flag tattoos were nearly twice as popular after September 11th as they were the year before. His is a no flab flag!

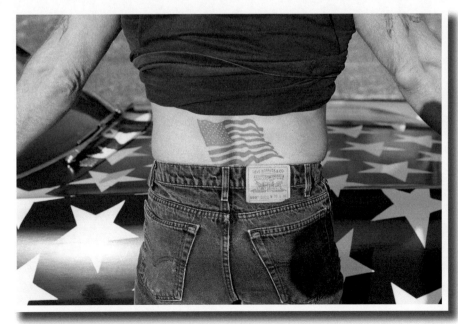

Virginia lost 85 people on 9/11.

Roll Model for Patriotism
Falls Church, Virginia, 2002

I was visiting a friend and decided to go for a stroll in his neighborhood when I met two Mormons who directed me to this classic 1974 Volkswagen Beetle. When I finally located the owner's home, Irvin, (1929 – 2015) handed me his business card, which stated, "Ambassador of Good Will for the Fire/EMS Department of Washington, D.C." Not only a visual statement—the car's stereo played patriotic tunes for the enjoyment of the neighbors. Irvin did not "roll over" after 9/11; he painted on his car the hero of Flight 93, Todd Beamer's battle cry, "Let's Roll!"

Teacher's Lesson in Patriotism
Fairfield, Connecticut 2002

A friend spotted this 1974 Volkswagen bus parked on a quiet, suburban street, but when we returned together to the neighborhood, it was gone. For a long time, we walked door to door, inquiring about it until we finally met the owner's daughter. She told us that her father Duke (1928 – 2018) had just left for his home down South, but would return. A third grade teacher for many years, he led his class in the "Pledge of Allegiance" to a traditional flag. If I were to grade the teacher's homemade flag bus, I would give him an "A."

Patriotic to the Core! New York City, the Apple of Our Eye
New York City 2001

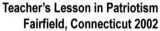

The Big Apple, the nickname for New York City, had its own and appropriate tribute right after 9/11 at Grand Central Station. An interesting historical fact, the terrorist attacks happened on 9/11, as well as Henry Hudson discovering Manhattan Island on September 11, 1609. Through the years, there have been various reasons for the tradition of young school children giving apples to their teachers; the fall apple harvest and as a form of respect and payment. Duke deserved an apple for his flag tribute.

**Barn with Cornfield
Dutchess County,
New York 2002**

Chris and his friend
Mike began painting
the barn the Friday
night after 9/11
and finished it
on Saturday.

Photo Credit *Farm Show Magazine*

**Ear of Corn Flag
Illinois 2011**

Duane Thompson
painted nearly 4,000
ears of corn for 18
years and shipped
them out to every
state in the Union.

In 2011, the website of Washington D.C.'s *National Journal* posted this photo in remembrance of 9/11.

Silo
Queen Anne's County, Maryland 2002

This 35-foot silo painted by painting contractors Pete and Faith after 9/11 has become a landmark for C-5 transport pilots on their approach to nearby Dover Air Force Base.

Left, Detail, 52-foot-by-100-foot Grain Silos Nebraska 2011

Iraq Marine Veteran's Silo Oswego County, New York 2011

13

Top, Bubba's Van...
Vanguard of Patriotism

Left, **This Artist is a Rock Star!**
Adair County, Iowa 2011

I had been driving for a long period of time on an interstate in western Iowa when I decided it was time to take a break. I stopped at a convenience store for a cup of coffee, and, as is my custom, asked the person at the counter if she had seen anything patriotic in the area. She said that in two exits, I could see the famous "Freedom Rock." A friend at work had told me about it a couple of years before, but I had forgotten about it. I came THAT close to missing it and would have been extremely disappointed had I not taken photos. I consider it another divine appointment! What are the odds? Ray (Bubba) was actually repainting the approximately 50-ton, 12-foot tall granite rock when I arrived. That year, he was paying tribute to SEAL Team Six and their successful mission in killing al-Qaeda terrorist leader Osama bin Laden. The rock also happens to be located near the birthplace of the actor, and patriot John Wayne, in Winterset, Iowa.

One person from Iowa died on 9/11.

One thousand-sixty-two people from New York State died on 9/11.

Rock Solid Patriotism Along a Highway
Connecticut 2013

Top, **America Rocks!**
St. Lawrence County, New York 2002

Bottom
Patriotism
Written in
Stone!
Bristol,
Connecticut
2017

This two-story bolder was painted by Terry and Julie, local college students, after 9/11 and is located in a desolate area near the Canadian border. Prior to 9/11 it had been covered with graffiti.

Ambulance
Virginia 2015

Engine Problems
Warren, Vermont 2010

Owned by the town doctor, this Cadillac hearse was continually getting sick along a parade route until it finally sprung a leak. This car serves as a metaphor for the state of our country. It needs the services of an ambulance. A band-aid is not going to do it. A tow truck could have helped (see the next page).

Red, Black & Blue
Connecticut 2011

**Tow Truck Hood
Queens, New York 2002**

*Two-hundred-fifty-seven
Queens residents died on 9/11.*

**Standing Out! Tow Truck Driver
with Mojo
Brooklyn, New York 2005**

A coworker had told me about a flag painted on the side of a van that sold flowers. When I arrived at the famous Green-Wood Cemetery in Brooklyn, I could not locate it. I was really disappointed after the long drive, but then, out of the corner of my eye red, white, and blue colors caught my attention. Right across the street was a tow truck at a McDonald's drive-through window. I ran to the driver named Angel and asked if I could take some shots. Before I could finish complimenting him on his truck, he jumped on top of the hood, providing me with a great shot. I liked his New York attitude in the pose and he didn't complain that I was interrupting his lunch. Angel also painted a 9/11 tribute mural near his home in Brooklyn.

Nine people from the town of Norwalk died on 9/11.

American Gothic
Norwalk, Connecticut 2002

Heath, pictured here with his wife Jennifer and daughter Melissa, had just put the finishing touches on the family's flag. A steel worker, he had cut out the stars himself at his welding shop. Betsy Ross is credited with designing this style of flag, which features the thirteen five-pointed stars arranged in a circle representing the thirteen colonies. This photo was one of many that I had on exhibit at my show at the Bruce Museum in 2013. For the ten-year anniversary of 9/11 it was also on exhibit at the Norwalk Museum.

After 9/11, Bruno, a Norwalk school custodian, made this flag out of metal.

18

Faith, Family, Country
Connecticut 2003

I decided to attend a Bible study one night, and, thanks to one of the attendees, I was able to get directions to this truck. The owner saw me taking photos and came out of his house to greet me. He spontaneously posed with his young family in the back of the truck. He also spray painted the word unity on his front hood next to the flag. Ironically, I had taken photos of this same truck parked on another street in Bridgeport a couple of months earlier. I was fortunate to capture this image, because I was down to my last few shots, having almost used up my last roll of film.

In 2006, Sara Reisman, an independent New York City based curator and former director for the New York City Department of Cultural Affairs' Percent for Art program chose this photo for a national group show in Poughkeepsie, New York.

A House United!
Orange County, New York 2005

In the Gospel of Mark 3:25, Jesus states, "And if a house be divided against itself, that house cannot stand" (King James version). This house serves as a metaphor for America after 9/11, when the country was pulling together. I was blessed with this picture after I helped an aspiring artist from Ukraine who needed a ride to submit her painting to an art show. A gallery goer there saw my patriotic photo of a food truck and thought I would like to know about this house. The owner, Bill, a house painter said he couldn't buy a flag after 9/11, so he decided to paint one on his house four days after the attacks. He recounted how disappointed he was after someone had actually "egged" it.

In 2009, curator Nan Rosenthal (1937–2014) of the Metropolitan Museum of Art, chose this photo for a group show at the Katonah Museum of Art. In 2007, Ted Mann, assistant curator from the Guggenheim Museum, chose this photo for a juried show in New Jersey. On 9/11/2011, it was published in the *New York Times* Metro Arts calendar.

> "It will be here until the day I die.
> I can guarantee it."
> —*Bill, June 11, 2005*

**Patriotic,
No Bones About It!
Connecticut 2012**

Top
**Family Flag
Florida 2009**

After 9/11, a military family living near Tampa had the side of their house painted with the flag. The father, William, has since retired from the Army Reserves. His son Trey has followed him in his footsteps and enlisted. The family is still intact, except sadly for Dreyfus, their golden retriever. In 2021, Elizabeth, the wife, told me, "We have no intention of painting it over!"

**Mickey's Dog House
Brigantine, New Jersey 2002**

I had to coax this Chihuahua out of his dog house with some dog bones that I had purchased at the local grocery store. I discovered this when I knocked on the door of the Mexican-American owner Tony, who also had a flag-themed van and cell phone.

21

Took a Double Take...
New York City 2001

This three-story, all-glass building, located on Fifth Avenue, was first wrapped with a huge 150-by-52-foot flag on October 13, 2001.
It was the idea of Israeli fashion designer Elie Tahari. If I had not attended a book signing in the city that night, I would have missed this amazing display. In 2003, this photo was on exhibit in New Jersey at a show titled "We Love NY: A Tribute to America."

Building Lights
Indianapolis, Indiana 2011

One person from Indiana died on 9/11.

Bottom
Artist's Truck
Staten Island, New York 2009
How many people drive a vehicle that
has both a flag and a picture of George
Washington attached to it?

Right
Mural
Staten Island,
New York 2020

One artist who doesn't mind lim-
iting his palette to just red, white
and blue. I caught Scot one day,
starting to paint a gas station roof
like a flag in his distinctive style.

One-hundred-ninety-two people from Staten Island died on 9/11

23

Fading Barn
Pennsylvania 2013

This barn is located about one-and-half-hours' drive from the 9/11 crash site of Shanksville, PA. I have photographed a Stars and Stripes: tiger, elephant, cat, dog, lion, cow, polar bear and a rather disrespectful flag-painted pig! I never got the chance to get the flag moose in Wisconsin. A professional equestrian named Renee and her family in Florida painted the flag right on a real horse. She said that after 9/11, "It was impossible to buy a flag." For the horse's safety she used clothing dye and shoe polish to paint the flag on both sides of the white horse.

Fading Horse
Connecticut 2009

Barn in the USA!
Chittenden County, Vermont 2004

After 9/11, there was a resurgence in flag-painted barns. The old ones were rehabilitated and painted with fresh coats of paint. Roger (1928 – 2018), who originally built and painted his barn, was employed for many years as a mail carrier. He also made a patriotic Uncle Sam mailbox to go along with his flag barn. Unfortunately, one of his Uncle Sam's was beheaded by vandals.

**Gravel Flag on Side of Highway
South Carolina 2009**

"The American flag represents all of
us and all the values we hold sacred."

—Adrian Cronauer

**Fake Flower Power Flag
Vernon, Connecticut 2006**

One-hundred-sixty-three people from Connecticut died on 9/11.

Budding Patriotism! Please No Plucking!
Purchase, New York 2002

Homegrown patriotism! Patriotism was blooming after 9/11. Domenick, the groundskeeper for a resort-hotel complex, used his red, white and blue thumb to plant this 20-by-30-foot tribute to the flag. Maybe he was inspired by a huge 6.65-acre flower flag that a seed company based in California planted in 2002.

One man from Purchase died on 9/11.

Keep Off the Grass!
Derby, Connecticut 2011

A real grass act! Adrian showed his true colors by spray painting his backyard.

In 2004, Karen Kienzle, curator of the DeSaisset Museum, chose this photo for a national group show in Santa Cruz, California.

A Toast to the Flag, Bar Façade
Luzerne County, Pennsylvania 2002

What's on tap? Cheers! Stan, a UPS driver by day and a tavern owner by night, painted this flag after 9/11. It was located about two hours from Ground Zero and four hours from Shanksville. I was able to photograph this one in time, but unfortunately, Bud's Tavern in Butte, Montana, was painted over when I arrived there.

Left
Shop Window Wine Bottle Flag
Stamford, Connecticut 2017

Ten Stamford residents died on 9/11.

28

Greg's House
Washington 2015

I drove 2,895 miles to meet Greg, a retired welder, who also painted the back of the house and his basketball backboard with the flag. Greg said, "We have all these freedoms here that we take for granted." He used 12 gallons of white paint, seven gallons of red and three gallons of blue. The stripes are 31 inches wide in red and white and the stars are each 24 inches tall. He could only fit 37 of the 50 stars.

Bottom,
Apartment House
Oklahoma 2010

Two people from Oklahoma died on 9/11.

Cowboy Boots
New Jersey 2002

Ladies Shoes
Connecticut 2011

Giving the Boot to Terrorists!
New York City 2002

This Vietnam War veteran let his
patriotism shine for all to see on one
of the busiest corners in the country,
near the New York City Public
Library and only about four miles
from Ground Zero. He probably had
red, white and blue shoe polish!
Bob told me that he had friends who
perished on 9/11. Sadly, I discovered
years later talking to another
shoeshiner on the corner that Bob
had passed away.

Manhattan lost 335 lives on 9/11.

Parking Booths
New York City 2002

After 9/11, Nelson, a parking booth attendant, painted three different booths with flags. He had time on his hands because he did not have any customers. The area was a no man's land. The above booth located on Church Street is just 12 blocks from Ground Zero. For weeks Nelson, a Dominican, suffered from a sore throat and the discomfort of breathing pollution from the blowing dust. Nelson knew the sad reason why some of his customers never returned for their cars. As I was talking to him, I was introduced to a friend of his named Dwight. He recounted to me his harrowing experience escaping from the 61st floor of one of the Twin Towers on his hands and knees, groping in the pitch dark, and finding the elevators just in time. Thank God, someone had waited and held the elevator door open for him.

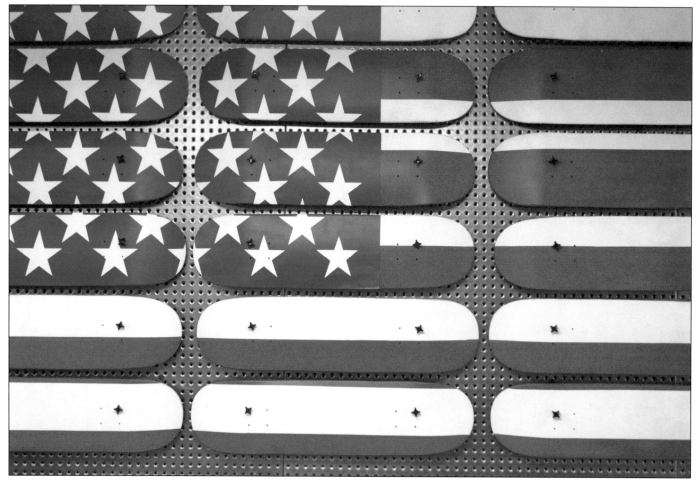

Front of Skateboards
New York City 2013

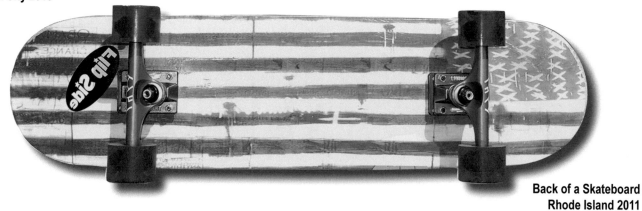

Back of a Skateboard
Rhode Island 2011

32

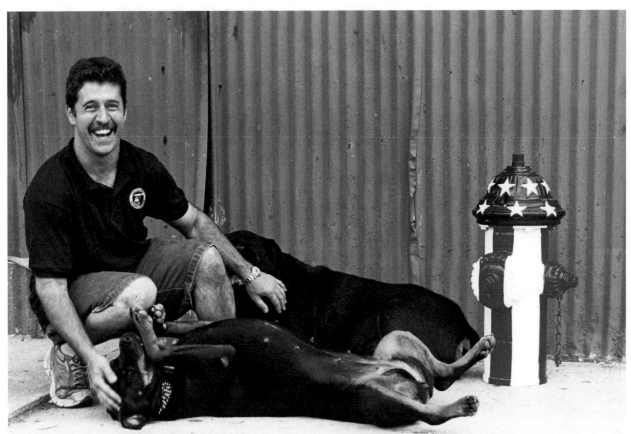

Fire Hydrant
Queens, New York 2002

John, an airbrush artist, painted this hydrant after 9/11. He forbid his two dogs, Odie and Lucy, from doing number one on his work of art. Somehow, he got a hold of a hydrant that was freestanding. Years later, he told me it is being used as a paper weight. He also painted his boat and van with flag motifs. I have photographed many flag fire hydrants across the country. A firefighter from West Haven, Connecticut, painted every single hydrant in the town red, white and blue with 9/11 inscribed on the top.

Fire House Dog Sculpture
by Billy Abshire
New York City Office Building Lobby 2003

A patriotic work of bark!

Fire Hydrant,
Stamford, Connecticut 2017

**Lady Liberty
Connecticut 2003**

Of the more than 69,386 pizza parlors in
the country this one stands out. I don't
consider it to be too cheesy.

**Flying Pizza Parlor Mural
Brooklyn 2015**

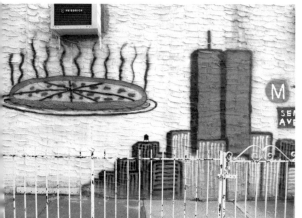

**Michael and
His Daughters
Stamford, Connecticut 2004**

The owner showing off his patriotic
pizza carton. No matter how you
slice it, a very patriotic family.

I came across a delicious recipe
in a Martha Stewart publication, on
how to make a pizza that looks
like an American flag using
tomatoes, cheese, and
blue potatoes.

In 2002, Joan Young, now head curator at The Solomon R. Guggenheim Museum of Art, chose this photo for a national exhibit in Poughkeepsie, New York.

Thinking Out of the Box!
West Haven, Connecticut 2002

I asked a police officer who was walking nearby if he had seen any interesting patriotic displays in the area. He told me about Ronnie's pizzeria. He recounted how depressed he had been after the unfolding events of September 11th. Late at night, sitting alone in his pizzeria, he dejectedly looked up at his pizza boxes stored on a shelf and then an inspiration came to him. He would put his empty pizza cartons to use to show his support for the country. He completed his project in the early morning hours of September 12, 2001. The photo above is of one of his workers. *A 50-year-old man from West Haven died on 9/11.*

Pizza Box
New York City 2017

After 9/11, flag images printed on pizza boxes were commonplace; however, this was the first time I saw the Freedom Tower displayed.

United We Stand Flag In Window
French Restaurant
New York City 2002

I have a personal connection with the WTC. My mother was a French chef and author of *Classics from a French Kitchen* published by Crown in 1983. She invited me to a memorable Les Dames d'Escoffier International, multi-course French feast in April of 1982 at the Windows on the World restaurant on the 107th floor of the North Tower of the World Trade Center. A lot of people avoided eating French food after France refused to join in the U.S.-led invasion of Iraq in 2003. Even the name French fries was changed to freedom fries on the U.S. Congressional cafeteria menu in Washington, D.C.

Pizzeria Patriotism
Bridgeport, Connecticut 2003

Fred, a talented African American former public school art teacher, was commissioned by the Turkish-born owner of this pizza and soul food restaurant to paint this mural. Situated in a rough neighborhood, even the local graffiti artists respected it! The artist also painted a flag mural on the façade of his home. Fred said in 2002 "Doing the Twin Towers will forever be a sad experience... I guess even a spiritual one."

Italy supported the U.S.-led war in Iraq. I'm glad they did — it would have been hard to boycott pizza!

A 25-year-old Bridgeport graduate student from India died on 9/11.

Above
Long, Long, May She Wave!
Springfield, Massachusetts 2010

Proportionally the longest painted flag I have encountered. Patriotism is on the menu and, of course, I had to leave a good tip! Diner owner at right.

No Small Potatoes
Connecticut 2002

After the French resisted supporting the U.S.-led war in Iraq in 2003, I just couldn't order French toast anymore. Instead, I enjoyed two eggs up with extra home fries. After a good cup of coffee, I was ready to hit the road again! America my cup — that runneth over!

Top, Ice Cream Shop, Ohio 2009
Left, Ice Cream Cartons, Connecticut 2006
Above, Ice Cream Cone Holder, New York 2004

38

Frank, Never Backpedaled When it Came to Patriotism!
Connecticut 2002

I was driving in downtown Norwalk, Connecticut, when I was startled by this senior citizen and his flags. I tried to catch up with him, but he disappeared in the traffic when I was stopped at a light. The next day, I canvased the neighborhood, finally locating his residence, a senior housing complex. Frank never married and was employed as a dishwasher, working for 30 years at my favorite Greek diner, the Family Diner.

Above, Peddler of Patriotism, Boy Scout
Darien, Connecticut 2004

It was the fourth bike Frank had owned during his lifetime and his favorite. He decked it out with flags, and other items: horn, radio, raccoon tail, dice, Florida license plate, Rolls Royce insignia, as well as other mementos. Years after I had first photographed him, I happened to be driving around town and noticed sadly in the back of a pickup truck what looked like his red bike. I knew something was wrong, and subsequently came across his obituary in the local paper. He passed away at the age of 80, on December 25, 2006. At his funeral, his bike was placed to the left of his open casket with all his flags. As mourners passed his casket they placed flowers in his bicycle's basket. I was fortunate though to have known this simple and gentle man who was the subject of one of my first flag-themed photographs. It was amazing timing that I was able to have had one last look at his beloved bicycle. Frank had a sweet tooth. On one of our last meetings, I took him out for an ice-cream cone, but that place was not as interesting or patriotic as the Ohio parlor on the previous page.

Below
Toy Styrofoam Airplanes
Connecticut 2015

1978 Cessna Seaplane at a Dock
Danbury, Connecticut 2003

This photo was one of many shots I had on exhibit at the Connecticut State Capitol in Hartford for the ten-year anniversary of 9/11.

Two Danbury residents died on 9/11.

Stars & Kites
Non-Patriots... Go Fly a Kite!
Toy Store
Middletown, Connecticut
2011

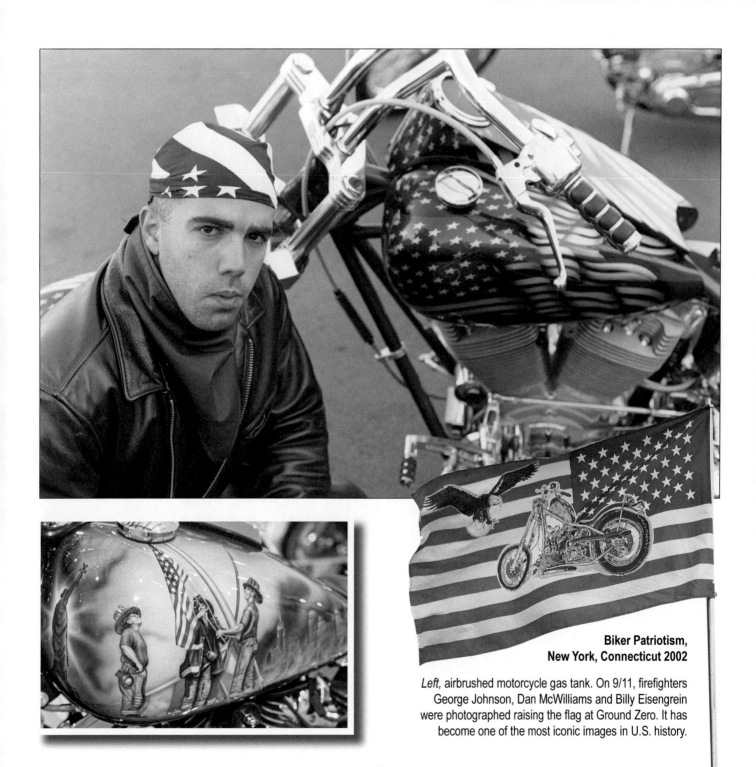

**Biker Patriotism,
New York, Connecticut 2002**

Left, airbrushed motorcycle gas tank. On 9/11, firefighters
George Johnson, Dan McWilliams and Billy Eisengrein
were photographed raising the flag at Ground Zero. It has
become one of the most iconic images in U.S. history.

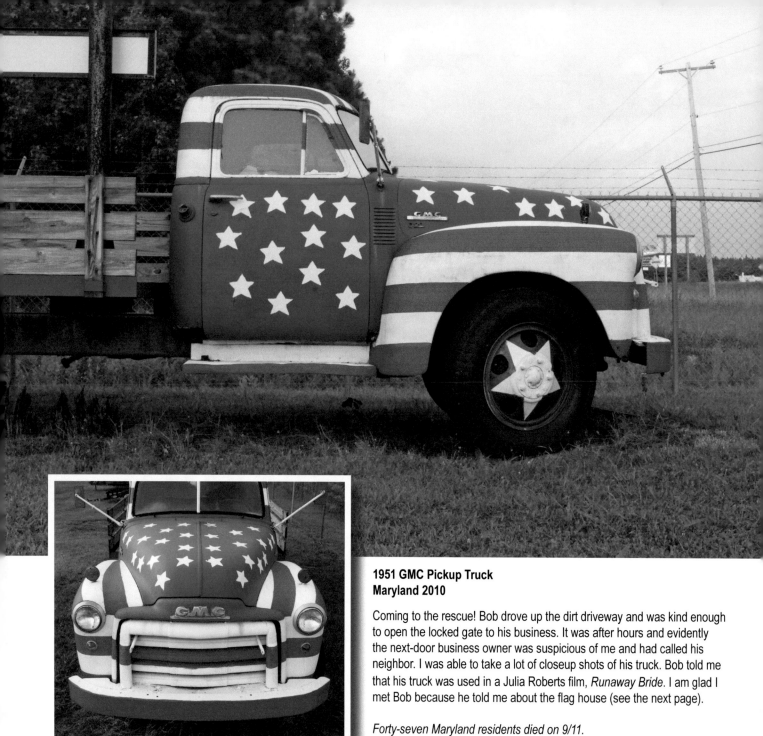

1951 GMC Pickup Truck
Maryland 2010

Coming to the rescue! Bob drove up the dirt driveway and was kind enough to open the locked gate to his business. It was after hours and evidently the next-door business owner was suspicious of me and had called his neighbor. I was able to take a lot of closeup shots of his truck. Bob told me that his truck was used in a Julia Roberts film, *Runaway Bride*. I am glad I met Bob because he told me about the flag house (see the next page).

Forty-seven Maryland residents died on 9/11.

Flag House
Maryland 2010

This photo was exhibited at the Star-Spangled
Banner Flag House Museum in Baltimore.

Beautician's Window Flag
Not Throwing Patriotism Out the Window!
Bridgeport, Connecticut 2002

After 9/11, a hair boutique in
California used actual human hair
to fashion a flag. A real beaut!

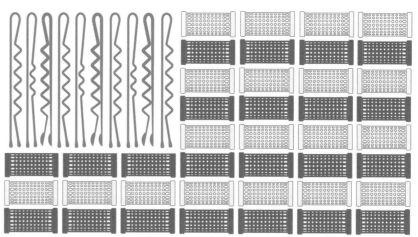

Red, White, and Blue
Bobby Pin and Hair Roller Flag
Darien, Connecticut 2021

By Robert Carley

**Barber's Flag
Connecticut 2013**

Michael's shop, a cut above with all
the patriotic trimmings!

**Red, White, and Blue Comb Flag
Darien, Connecticut 2021**

By Robert Carley

For 20 years, I have combed the
country looking for flags.

Flag Shutters
Michigan 2013

Michigan lost two residents on 9/11.

Flagstone Front Door Entrance
Darien, Connecticut 2010

Flag Hand Railing to
Front Door of a Small House
Ohio 2013

Ohio lost one resident on 9/11.

Right Place... Right Time
Michigan, July 4th, 2009

After taking many shots of this house in a small town, I started off to my next destination. But as I was driving, I heard that still, small voice saying, "turn back." I thought it had to be an irrational thought. But after wrestling with it, I gave in and made a U-turn and headed back to the house. A few minutes passed when, from the corner of my eye, I noticed an old, blue van. It stopped behind my car. Curious, I walked over to it, when all of a sudden, five flag-attired people jumped out. I excitedly grabbed my camera and got them posed with the flag house in the background. The woman even had Lady Liberty sunglasses that matched the Lady Liberty painted on the side of the house. I asked what had brought them here. Amazingly, and conveniently for me, they had a flat tire in front of the flag house. Talk about a divine appointment!

"The marvels of daily life are exciting; no movie director can arrange the unexpected that you find in the street."

—*Photographer Robert Doisneau*

In 2011, Daniel Belasco, then curator at the Jewish Museum, chose this award-winning photo for inclusion in a group show called "Brush with Fate" in Greenwich, Connecticut. Also in 2011, Tom Eccles, executive director of Bard College's curatorial studies program, chose this photo for the "Art of the Northeast" show in New Canaan, Connecticut.

Top Right, New York Stock Exchange, Holiday Lights, 11 Wall Street, New York City 2008

The New York Stock Exchange is only an 11 minute walk to where the Twin Towers once stood.

Above, a flag that was popular with the Occupy Wall Street movement. It was photographed in Cambridge, Massachusetts, in 2014.

In 2009, a disability rights activist was displaying this flag in New Haven, Connecticut. In 2011, Joan Young, associate curator of contemporary art, Guggenheim Museum, now the director, curatorial affairs, chose this photo for a national group show at the New Jersey Center for Visual Arts in Summit, New Jersey.

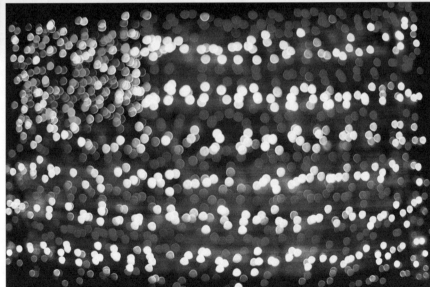

"Essentially what photography
is is life lit up."

—Photographer Sam Abell

Top
America, a Beacon of Hope!
New York City 2012

America letting her light shine! About 360,000 pedestrians a day see this LED flag, which I have photographed in the heart of Times Square multiple times through its various incandescent incarnations. This 520-square-foot, blast-proof glass Army recruiting station has been at this location since 1948. It is about a 3.8-mile walk to Ground Zero and is the best and brightest neon sign in a sea of neon signs and billboards, worthy of this location's nickname, the "Crossroads of the World."

Right, Detail of a Light Bulb on a Billboard
Brooklyn, New York 2011

Left, Homemade Light Flag
Norwalk, Connecticut 2002

I photographed this homemade holiday light display in front of a restaurant, purposely out of focus. It was chosen by Robert Rosenblum (1927 – 2006) of the Solomon R. Guggenheim Museum for inclusion in the Viridian Artists, (Chelsea) 13th Annual National Juried Exhibition in 2002.

Flag-Gas Pump, High-Octane Patriotism!
Louisiana 2010

One person from this state died on 9/11.

Raw Patriotism, Septic Pump Tanker
Texas 2010

Fill 'er up! Jimmie and Maria, through the years, have owned several flag-decorated, septic-tank trucks. Some people might think that the idea of painting a flag on something to do with septic tanks STINKS or that it goes against the National Flag Code. I disagree. I know them and they love America.

It's backing up! Time to get one of those septic-vacuum trucks to clean up Washington, D.C. It's a cesspool!

Oil Tanker at Gas Station
Mississippi 2011

Built Like a Tank!
Stonington, Connecticut 2021

My road trip to Stonington, on the border of Rhode Island, was a trip during a time of a pandemic. I had to wear the face mask on the left at rest stops and restaurants on the way. I did not get too close to Charlie who told me that he had time on his hands during the 2020 COVID-19 lock down to restore and paint his '48 Chevy delivery van. I used my zoom lens to keep six feet away. These old cars were built to last.

Stonington lost one 42-year-old man on 9/11.

Tank
New Jersey 2009

I was tankful to find this, right in New Jersey, where it was parked in front of a National Guard office. A full tank of patriotism! *Six-hundred-seventy-four New Jersey residents died on 9/11.*

Above, Lobster Boat
Maine 2010

I nearly missed the boat! When I arrived at this small fishing port, the flag lobster boat that I wanted to photograph was anchored far away from the docks. A kind fisherman took me out on his boat so that I could get close enough to take some good shots.

Fish Market Display
Rowayton, Connecticut 2015

A 48-year-old man from Rowayton died on 9/11.

Making Waves, Speed Boat
City Island, Bronx, New York 2005

These days too many people are throwing patriotism overboard. What a way to wave the flag!

Ninety-one people from the Bronx lost their lives on 9/11.

In 2006, this photo (top) was exhibited in "Defining Freedom," a juried show at Eastern Washington University in Cheney, Washington.

Patriotism Bottoming Out
Brigantine, New Jersey 2003

A 46-year-old woman from this town died on 9/11.

Dart, Connecticut 2009

A patriotic work of dart that hits the bull's-eye

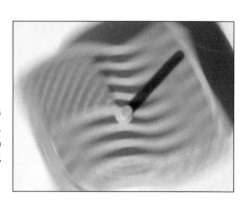

New Spins on the Flag... Toy Top Connecticut 2004

Toothpick Connecticut 2017

Bead Flag Shanksville, Pennsylvania 2009

I photographed this small flag placed on a fence along with other makeshift tributes, before the permanent memorial was built.

Butterfly The Metamorphosis of the Flag Connecticut 2004

**Fanning the Flames
of Patriotism
Connecticut 2002**

A low tech fan. The flag goes
Asian — it was probably even
made in China. Ewa was a college
student from Poland.

"Spontaneously a wave of

patriotism unseen since

World War II fanned out

across our nation...

Within hours, Walmart

and mom-and-pop stores

sold out of flags."

—*Historian Douglas Brinkley*

on 9/11/2001

**A High Tech Hand-Held
Battery-Powered Light Fan
Connecticut 2009**

Home Sweet Home Cookie Jar
New York City Diner, 2017

Cookies
New York City
Bakery 2015

That's the Way the Cookie Crumbles
Falls Church, Virginia 2002

"That's the last time I will leave you two alone!" This was the amusing response from the mother of the teenager when she first saw in her driveway the new flag paint job on their 1992 Ford Ranger. This was a collaboration between a father, William, and his daughter, showing their love of country after 9/11. This truck was used to deliver Girl Scout Cookies to a local Air Force base for personnel on their way to fight in Afghanistan. This home is located about ten miles from where American Airlines Flight 77 hit the Pentagon on 9/11. An amazing coincidence of history, ground was broken to begin construction at the Pentagon on 9/11/1941.

Two women from Falls Church lost their lives on 9/11.

Practice Makes Perfect, Corvette and Old Truck
Trumbull, Connecticut 2004 and Norwalk, Connecticut 2002

One winter day, I started out searching for a flag-painted snowplow that a friend had told me about, but ended up finding something better. I had called Leo's auto body shop because I thought that the owner, Raymond (1949 - 2005), might have seen it or had actually painted it. He had never seen the plow, but nonchalantly told me that he had just painted his sports car like a flag. I had previously photographed his big, old truck when it was parked in front of his business. Regarding his first flag and his patriotism he said, "These feelings prompted me to create a symbol of patriotism of the American flag flying proudly on the largest item that we had at Leo's to be seen by passersby."

Two men from Trumbull died on 9/11.

Flag House
Pennsylvania 2010

This was painted in honor of Engine 55, a firehouse located in lower Manhattan. It was one of the first responding units on 9/11. A plaque in front of this house states "Dedicated to those who gave their lives for freedom." On the roof, the owner painted, in giant letters, "GOD BLESS AMERICA."

Pennsylvania lost 30 of its residents on 9/11.

In 2011, Elisabeth Sussman, a curator from the Whitney Museum of American Art, chose this photo for inclusion in the Viridian Artists' 1st International Juried Photography Exhibition in Chelsea, New York City. Also in 2011, Fred Adelson, an art history professor, chose this photo for a group show at the Perkins Center for the Arts in Moorestown, New Jersey. The *Philadelphia Inquirer* posted it along with their online article about the exhibit. In 2010, Steven Assael, well-known painter and teacher at the School of Visual Arts, chose this photo for a group exhibit in Ridgefield, Connecticut.

Patriotism Through the Roof!
Delaware 2002

Not only did Americans hit the roof in anger after 9/11, they painted them too! On the flight path to Dover Air Force Base, the barn's owner, Clarence, said that pilots sometimes dipped a wing as a salute when they flew by.

Delaware lost one resident on 9/11.

Bottom, Roof
Maine 2006

After 9/11, Americans knew the importance of unity. We realized that we were all going to go under if we didn't realize we all lived "under the same roof."

Maine lost three residents on 9/11.

Gate
Connecticut 2010

In the King James version of the Bible the text reads: "Because straight is the gate, and narrow is the way, which leadeth unto life, and few there be that find it."

In 1776, our Founding Fathers took the narrow gate, in creating a new kind of government that was an experiment in democracy.

**Walter's T-Shirt
Connecticut 2002**

I spotted this house painter's T-shirt in my neighborhood as he was walking to work.

Bottom
**Jesus Saves T-Shirt
Connecticut 2002**

Photo taken at a Christian bookstore.

**Looking to the Cross
Connecticut 2004**

Immediately after 9/11, church attendance surged by around 25 percent. I was inspired when I saw at Ground Zero a 17-foot-high cross-section of steel I-beams that formed a cross. It gave people hope.

Don't Tread on Me

JESUSAVES

The "Jug Lady" (1933 - 2015)
Mays Landing, New Jersey 2002

Following the suggestion of a local radio station after 9/11, Josephine created a flag display with almost a thousand red, white and blue one-gallon milk and kitty litter jugs. Prior to 9/11, Josephine, a school bus driver, had made other designs out of the jugs: rabbits, Santa Clauses, etc. She received the support of neighbors, who chipped in and contributed their "empties." How did she color them? One day someone stopped by her house to suggest she use food dye to color the jugs, which was a lot faster and easier than painting. The display showed her patriotism and also had another purpose, but not so noble — to keep kids and trucks like the one on the next page, off her grass. Thanks to a contact I had from the Smithsonian Museum in Washington, D.C., I was able to locate this flag.

No Refuge for the Refuse!
Trashing Bin Laden
Norwalk, Connecticut 2004

Fairfield lost three young men on 9/11.

I regretted not driving to Kansas to take photos of a flag house. It was my vacation, and I had too many things to do! I felt much better though later in the week when I spotted this garbage truck exiting the highway in my hometown. Running red lights, I was able to flag down Andrew, the driver. In fact, a couple of friends had already told me about it. This was an even more unique patriotic display than a flag-painted house! Sadly, when I did end up driving to Kansas, the flag house had been painted over two weeks before I arrived.

Trashing the Flag;
Not Throwing Away Their Patriotism!
Fairfield, Connecticut 2002

After 9/11, a Boy Scout Troop's tribute to the flag was placed in front of a public-school building. They violated the National Flag Code, but their hearts were in the right place.

Patriotism Unchained!
New York 2005

"Boots," an ex-Marine, placed this flag made out of nuts and chains in front of a tattoo shop, where I discovered it on my drive to West Point, New York. It was one of many he made at his home in Stormville, New York after 9/11. He also fastened one to the front bumper of his van. He noticed other people would lose their traditional fabric flags from their vehicles. He said the advantage of his was that it would never fly off. A welder by trade for 35 years, he was employed by the railroad company Metro North. He put these skills to work artistically, exhibiting other chain flags at a gallery that featured "biker art." With the flag, above, he tried to make it as proportionally accurate to a real flag as possible. His friends would give him grief if he was too far off.

In 1776, America was a "trial balloon" for democracy. The high-minded Founding Fathers never foresaw how high she would soar.

Left Page Bottom
Showing Our Metal! Steel Flag
Wilton, Connecticut 2002

Rick, a professional metal sculptor, made this flag, which was placed for a time in front of the Wilton Public Library.

On 9/11, Dave Karnes, an accountant and former Marine, drove from his office in Wilton to the WTC and rescued two people from the rubble.

Four men from Wilton died on 9/11.

Car Dealership
Connecticut 2010

Top, Rising to New Heights!
Hot Air Balloon Show
Goshen, Connecticut 2003

America always rises to the occasion and many of her critics are full of hot air! America is not perfect, but too many people enjoy deflating America's many accomplishments.

One resident of Goshen died on 9/11.

Patriotism More Than Skin Deep!
Everett, Washington 2011

Sam (1950 – 2020) welcomed me with open arms when I arrived at his house from Connecticut after a long 2,900 mile drive. On this road trip, I consumed about eighty-three gallons of gas, ten Big Macs, nine vanilla milkshakes, five Whoppers, seven McDonald's breakfast burritos and five gallons of coffee extra light no sugar.

Sam proudly gave me a tour of his home where every day was the 4th of July!

Sam wanted to keep the memory of 9/11 alive and showed me the poster below which he had made.

A few years after my visit, sadly his wife passed away and he had to sell this house.

66

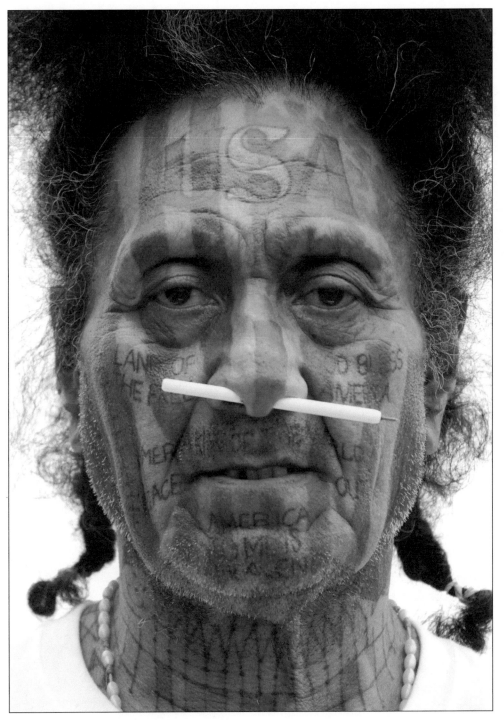

An Uncle Sam, With a Polynesian Accent!

He and his old dog "Blue" were forced to move into a motor home that he parked in a relative's driveway.

He grew up poor in Tonga, a Polynesian kingdom in the South Pacific.

A stowaway on a boat headed for California, he arrived on U.S. shores at the age of 17 hoping for a better life. Eventually he found work on a fishing boat in Alaska and then at a fish processing plant in Everett, Washington, where he cut up and packaged salmon and crab.

He ended his last years hanging out most mornings at an intersection near a gas station where he became well known and loved in the community for waving his flags and voicing his patriotism. He didn't do it for money, he said, but he appreciated the small tokens people gave him, especially peanut butter.

"If they give me money, I tell them, 'Give it to God.' "

"America is the best country in the world!" and "America to me is heaven," were his common refrains.

Driving home from my 2011 visit, I thought for a moment — in honor of Sam — that I should get a tattoo too!

The photo on the left was exhibited in 2011 at the Mills Pond House Gallery, St. James, New York, in an exhibit titled "American Mosaic, Celebrating Our Country's Diversity."

67

Paul's Automobile Mechanic's
Custom Decorated Tool Box
Pennsylvania 2018

Mechanic's Flag With Wrenches and Bolts

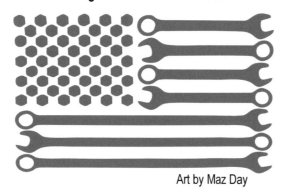

Art by Maz Day

Screwdriver
Connecticut 2012

A handy tool for dealing with your nutty anti-American
friends who have a few screws loose.

Keep On Trucking!
Maine 2010

After taking photos of the truck pictured above at a gas station, I soon realized that it was not the truck that I had originally set out for. It was a bonus shot and I was able to meet the owner named Heath. The one that I had been told about by the lobster boat captain was located about two minutes down the road. An artist named Jay painted the old truck. "My truck, runneth over!" What were the chances that I would find two flag-painted trucks so close to each other?

Home of the Brave
Minnesota 2013

Gary was pestered by an unhappy neighbor with questions about when he was going to paint the flag over. His defiant response, "Never!" It took him three weeks to paint it after 9/11. I will always remember my time in Minneapolis, where I spent one sleepless night at a Walmart parking lot because I could not get a hotel room. It was amazing how much activity there was at that parking lot! After that experience, I had more appreciation for all the cheap hotels I had stayed in.

Close call
Missouri 2010

I found out about this house inadvertently, when I visited a friend who was on the phone with someone from Missouri. I was put on the phone with her and she told me about this house. Unfortunately, when I arrived no one was home. I would have loved to photograph the owner, but I was still very happy to photograph the house, because flag houses are very hard to find.

Two people from Missouri died on 9/11.

Eight residents of Illinois died on 9/11.

The Handwriting Is on the Wall, Justice Will Prevail!
Palatine, Illinois 2006

I was exhibiting one of my flag photos at a gallery in Chicago, near this town. During my phone call to the gallery administrator there, I was asked if my photograph on display of a flag house was the one in the neighboring town of Palatine. She continued to tell me about another flag house that I had an opportunity to photograph for my collection. I was able to meet Douglas, the owner, a professional roofer, and his dog Maco. Douglas told me he went to work one day and upon his return his house had been painted by his wife, Renee, with the red, white and blue because she couldn't buy a flag after 9/11. For maintenance reasons, Douglas told me that he was just about to remove the 10-foot-by-22-foot flag. It was worth my 1,724 mile round-trip journey!

In 2007, this photo was exhibited in Lawrence, Massachusetts, in a group show called "Honoring Memory: Recalling 9/11 and Other Travesties of Humanity."

Bird House
Wilton, Connecticut, 2002

**Parking Meter
York, Pennsylvania 2013**

I took photos before my
chance had expired.

**Detail of a Mickey Mouse T-Shirt
Milford, Connecticut 2003**

It reminds me of the shape
of the meter.

**God Bless America Watch
Connecticut 2006**

Ticking off our enemies! America keeps
on taking a licking but keeps on ticking.
I had to keep an eye on the time so that
I could keep feeding the parking meter,
pictured on the left.

Patriotic Pavement, No Passing on Patriotism! Rhode Island 2020

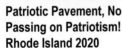

America paving the way! The patriotic road less traveled can be bumpy, but it's the one that leads in the right direction. Some of my most enjoyable times in my life were my flag trips with the open road in front of me. I felt freedom. One of my favorite car CD's — Willie Nelson's, "On the Road Again!"

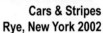

**Cars & Stripes
Rye, New York 2002**

I'm sold! Chris, a former Chrysler/Dodge car salesman, put in eight hours to paint his classic 1977 Cadillac Seville. He custom-ordered the decal letters that were placed on the front and rear windows. I would have loved to drive this cool car cross country on a flag photo trip. I had to settle for rental cars for my trips because I wasn't sure if my old Dodge Caravan could handle the grueling nonstop 12-hour days. I only got one speeding ticket in all my years of traveling in the state of Nebraska. In 2002, I discovered MapQuest, which was a breakthrough for me. That navigation tool gave me confidence and the ability to calculate how many hours it would take to get to each location. I'd print out my whole trip with step-by-step directions. It's great now to have GPS on my cellphone, although when I used to get lost, that's when I'd find some amazing flags.

Five people from Rye died on 9/11.

Stars and Bites Food Truck
Beacon, New York 2004

One person from Beacon died on 9/11.

Robert's hot dog truck really cut the mustard!
Robert (1934 - 2006) didn't offer French's Dijon style mustard or
hummus. He would have loved the ketchup bottle with the picture of
George Washington and the bag of chips on the left. This company
was really chipping in with patriotism. Because France was not sup-
portive in the second Gulf War, Americans stopped calling French fries
"French." "Freedom fries" was the preferred alternative. In 2006, artist
Mel Leipzig chose this photo for inclusion in a group show in Trenton,
New Jersey called "My America."

**Flag Man
Queens, New York 2003**

Luis cheerfully greeted me with "I love America," in a Spanish accent. Pointing to the cars speeding by and honking, he said, "These are my people." Looking like he was dressed up for work, laughing and smiling he said, "This strip of land is my office. They are my customers." That morning, thanks to a tip from a coworker, I jumped in my car and drove as fast as I could to the La Guardia airport area and on my third try, caught him at what he curiously described as "spot 80."

In 2003, Tumelo Mosaka, formerly, assistant curator of contemporary art, Brooklyn Museum of Art, chose this photo for a national group show in Poughkeepsie, New York. In 2004, Charlotta Kotik, former head of the department of modern and contemporary art at the Brooklyn Museum, chose this photo for a group show at the New Jersey Center for Visual Arts. In 2005, it was part of another group show at the Katonah Museum of Art. In 2008, well-known photojournalist Paul Fusco of Magnum Photos chose it for a group show in New Canaan, Connecticut.

Left, **Beach Inflatable Inner Tube**
Weed Beach, Connecticut 2017

Keeping Watch
Florida 2010

In a drowning world America is still the world's lifeguard! I discovered this near Miami on South Beach. I found the inflatable life preserver tube at a chandlery in New Jersey in 2011. It also serves as a metaphor, the U.S. — the world's life preserver. After 9/11 terrorists insulted America, calling us the "Great Satan." In reality, judging from all the federal and private foreign aid programs, one could metaphorically call America, the "Good Samaritan." In 2019 the U.S. government spent $39.2 billion on foreign aid. According to statistics, the American people are among the most generous in the world.

76

Riding A Red, White & Blue Wave of Patriotism
Atlantic City, New Jersey 2003

What better way for a busy fireman to relieve his stress than to get out in the sun and surf! This 9 foot surfboard served Doug well, finally wearing out after 20 years. He recounted the "surreal" experience of being at Ground Zero just a few days after the Towers collapsed. When we met, he had mentioned a flag made out of seashells that he had seen on a beach. Thanks to a waitress at a diner, I was able to locate it in 2011. Below is a photo of one of my favorite FDNY firetrucks photographed in 2003. I bet Doug would have loved to catch a ride on this one.

Mailbox,
Vista, New York
2007

Top, Mailman, Connecticut 2002

After 9/11, I even started getting Stars and
Stripes designed junk mail! This nice
mailman, Danny, also showed off his flag
socks to me.

Bottom, Mailbox
9/11 Leaving its Stamp on America
Connecticut 2003

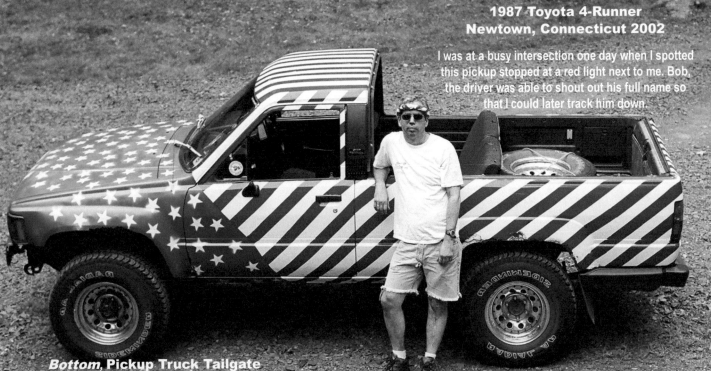

1987 Toyota 4-Runner
Newtown, Connecticut 2002

I was at a busy intersection one day when I spotted this pickup stopped at a red light next to me. Bob, the driver was able to shout out his full name so that I could later track him down.

Bottom, **Pickup Truck Tailgate**
Darien, Connecticut 2006

An airbrushed rendering of the Pentagon and the American flag with a United We Stand license plate.

CONNECTICUT
911·US
UNITED WE STAND

Cement Mixer
Brooklyn, New York 2005

This truck, owned by Tony, put a new spin on the flag. Dean, a business associate of mine, saw this truck on a highway and tried to get photos of it while driving. He excitedly showed me the truck the next day, but without the full name of the company. I tried calling cement companies in the area to track it down, but was unsuccessful. The next week, Dean was able to find another photo that thankfully had the full company name. In 2005, Roosevelt University's Gage Gallery exhibited this photo in a group show called "Freedom: Response."

One-hundred-eighty-three people from Brooklyn died on 9/11.

***Top*, "Gone But Not Forgotten..."**
Bronx, New York 2002

I was taking photos of murals around City Island in the Bronx, when I stopped to talk to a woman on the sidewalk who was wheeling her baby in a stroller. I asked her if she had seen any patriotic displays in the area. To my delight, she told me about a car show being held at the nearby Orchard Beach parking lot. With the one-year anniversary of 9/11, I photographed many WTC-themed paint jobs that day. This 1957 Chevy was owned at that time by Walt from Auburn, New York.

Stars and Stripes 1968 Impala
Orchard Beach, New York 2002

This classic Chevy convertible, owned by Anthony of Pelham, New York was also in the show and was professionally painted by his brother Victor in his shop. Anthony has many fond memories of his daughter Julianne, who enjoyed riding with the top down listening to music and even feeding birds that followed them.

Mural Queens, New York 2009

In 2009, Paul Master-Karnik, formerly director of the De Cordova Museum, chose this photo for a group show in Greenwich, Connecticut.

"It is an illusion that photos are made with a camera... they are made with the eye, heart and head."

—*Henri Cartier Bresson*

Mural Massachusetts 2013

American Flight 11 and United Flight 175 were hijacked after leaving Boston's Logan Airport on 9/11. One of the 9/11 leaders, Khalid Sheikh Mohammed, envisioned 12 hijacked planes, one of which was supposed to crash into Boston's Prudential Tower.

Massachusetts lost 92 people on 9/11.

Detail, Mural at a Hardware Store
Crown Heights, Brooklyn, New York 2015

This 2014 mural is dedicated to Captain Vernon A. Richard whose portrait is included in the mural. It is also dedicated to all the FDNY and NYPD responders who sacrificed their lives on 9/11. As of 2021, it is still there but obstructed. It is interesting to see the different creative renderings of the Twin Towers. One of the most moving WTC murals I have seen is one I spotted in 2015 while driving through a small Montana town. This demonstrated to me the emotional hit Americans took after 9/11, even in a remote town in Montana.

Left, Mural, Ghostlike Towers
Brooklyn, New York 2011

Detail, Mural, Photo in the 9/11 Museum Collection
New York City, 2002

The photo on the left was one of 18 of my photos that were exhibited at the New York State Museum in Albany in a group exhibit reflecting on the ten-year anniversary of 9/11.

Bales of Hay
Newtown, Connecticut 2015

Discovering this was like finding a needle in a haystack!

Stone Wall Flag
Connecticut 2017

84

Public Bus, Patriots Are Not Thrown Under the Bus!
Danbury, Connecticut 2002

Non-patriots are sent to the back of the bus!

Top, **Truck Stop, North Carolina 2014**

The exact moment I was pulling out of a restaurant on my way to the on-ramp of the highway, this tractor trailer, owned by Larry, was coming down the exit ramp heading to a truck stop. It then proceeded to a truck wash so that I had a squeaky-clean truck to take photos of.

Bottom, **Pallet Company Truck**
Paterson, New Jersey 2002

A 9/11 terrorist who lived in Paterson was one of the five hijackers on board of American Airlines Flight 77.

Two Paterson residents died on 9/11

Left, **Pallet**
Connecticut 2002

"Sure I wave the American flag. Do you know a better flag to wave? Sure I love my country with all her faults. I'm not ashamed of that, never have been, never will be."

—*Actor John Wayne*

Zero Dark Thirty (2012)
A Great 9/11 Inspired Movie! A chronicle of the decade-long hunt for al-Qaeda terrorist leader Osama bin Laden after the September 2001 attacks, and his death at the hands of the Navy S.E.A.L.s Team 6 in May 2011.

Four people from Texas died on 9/11.

Movie Theatre Marquee Fairfield, Connecticut 2011

Drive-In Movie Theatre, Patriotism Now Playing! Briscoe County, Texas 2010

There's nothing like movie-theatre pop corn in a big tub with a lot of butter! So, I was disappointed when I arrived at this theatre built in 1955 because it was closed, and maybe, by the looks of it, for a long time. A John Wayne western might even have been one of the last movies to play here!

One person from Bedford died on 9/11.

Oldsmobile
Bedford, New York 2004

WATER WIZARD

I first spotted this sedan parked across the street from my workplace in Greenwich, Connecticut. I left a note on the windshield, but the owner never got back to me. Driving home from a church meeting one day, I spotted the car again, parked on the side of the road next to a row of businesses. I went store to store and was able to meet the young lady who owned the car.

***Far Left,* Car Wash
Bradenton, Florida 2014**

9/11 terrorists took flying lessons in Venice, Florida less than hour from this car wash.

Four people from Florida died on 9/11.

***Left,* Car Air Freshener
Connecticut 2004**

***Left,* Car
Connecticut 2006**

87

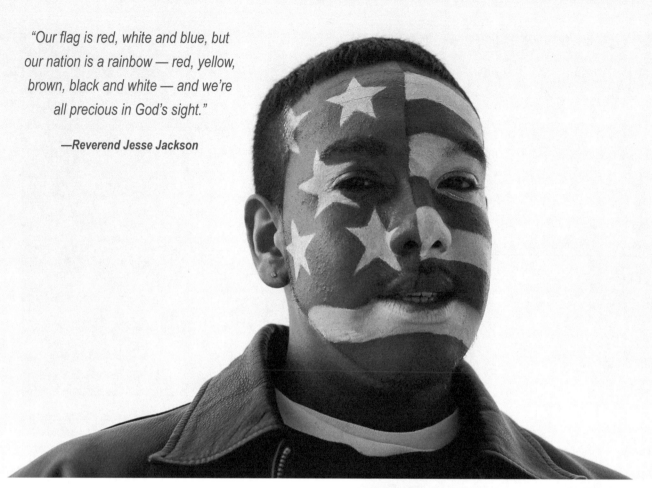

"Our flag is red, white and blue, but our nation is a rainbow — red, yellow, brown, black and white — and we're all precious in God's sight."

—Reverend Jesse Jackson

**Father's Canvas, His Son Ray's Face
Meriden, Connecticut 2002**

Face Painting
Vermont 2010

88

Flag Hoodie
Stamford, Connecticut 2015

The lack of knowledge among the young about American history is alarming. If we don't do something about it, I expect future generations to confuse 9/11 with 7-Eleven!

Emotional Ties
Norwalk, Connecticut 2002

Since 9/11, I have photographed many patriotic ties, including this one worn by Edgar who worked as a cashier at my local grocery store. The photo on the left was one of many exhibited at the Museum of Connecticut History in Hartford.

Old Carriage House Turned into a Barn
Bristol County, Massachusetts 2006

Originally, I set out to take photos of a flag-painted truck that was going to be in a parade. I could not find a parking spot close to the parade route and was forced to park several blocks away. That worked out well, however, because right in the front yard of the house where I was parked, was a flag-painted jeep. After the parade, I hitched a ride with Bruce, who drove me back to my car. We struck up a conversation, and he mentioned that he had actually painted his barn like a flag (Above). After feeling satisfied that I had taken enough photos of his barn, I drove off. As I was driving, I heard that still, small voice nudging me to drive back to the barn. I wrestled with the idea, then I made a U-turn and drove back.

Flag House
Bristol County, Massachusetts 2006

This was the same situation that I had experienced in Michigan with the flag-painted house. As I entered a coffee shop, I asked one departing customer if she had seen any other patriotic images similar to the barn across the street. Her suspicious father sitting in his parked car overheard our conversation and called me over. He said, to my amazement, that he just so happened to have noticed a flag painted house that morning! I was able to speak to the owner, Marie, who told me she painted the house like a flag after her young daughter got the idea because they were not able to buy a flag after 9/11. In 2007, Valerie Smith, director of exhibitions at the Queens Museum of Art, selected this photo for the 58th "Art of the Northeast" juried show in New Canaan, Connecticut.

A fence I found on the way to the house.

91

In 2006, this photo was in a train exhibit in St. Louis, Missouri. Bonnie Stutski, photo editor of *Smithsonian Magazine,* was the juror.

Patriots All Aboard!
New York 2005

I was on the right track when I found this caboose on my way to take photos of something else. On 9/11 a friend of mine living in my hometown watched ash-covered commuters who had fled New York exiting the trains at our local station. Known as a New York City commuter town, Darien lost six men on 9/11. I remember a moving 9/11 kiosk set up right in Grand Central with photos and names of victims. Many of these commuters never returned to Grand Central Station for their train home.

Retired Train Conductor's Flag
Middlebury, Vermont 2002

I was driving up Route 7, when this flag stopped me in my tracks. George (1917-2011) made it right after 9/11. I also like his polkadot railroad hat.

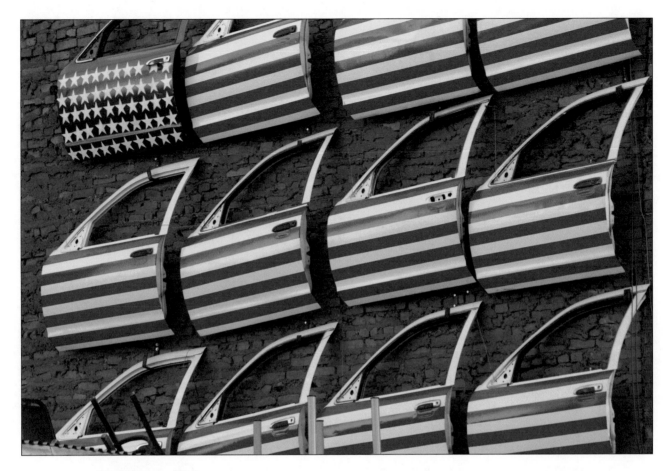

Car Doors on a Wall
Brooklyn, New York 2013

I was working as a background actor, being transported by van to a television set with other extras, when I happened to look up at the side of a building and discovered one of the most off-the-wall displays I have ever seen. It nearly blew my doors off!

Car Door with the Twin Towers
Orchard Beach, Bronx, New York 2002

The owner of this 1963 Buick Special, Jose, also painted the hood of the car with the iconic Ground Zero firefighters raising the flag.

"Pulling Together" Pickup Truck
Woodbury, New York 2002

This rare 1964 Chevrolet Corvair was painted by Gregg, a professional chainsaw artist. One of the reasons he painted it was because some-one stole the flag that he had placed on his front yard. On September 12, 2001, his mother and other members of the family started painting it. His finishing touch was placing one of his works, a wooden fireman bear, in the back of the truck. It brought back to me my childhood memories of my mother's white 1961 Corvair.

One 44-year-old man from Woodbury died on 9/11.

Pickup Truck T-Shirt
Rest Stop, Pendleton, Oregon 2015

One 32-year-old man from Oregon died on 9/11.

94

Stars and Strikes Dodge Ram 50 Pickup
Major League Patriotism!
Port Chester, New York 2004

Thomas, a baseball coach and social studies teacher, hit a home run when he painted his truck like a flag after 9/11. This photo serves as a metaphor for the country today. Americans need to remember: Don't be mean — we're all on the same team! So we don't strike out, this is what we should have learned after 9/11. America should stick to the game plan! Teamwork! Teamwork! Teamwork!

In 2004, the photo above was exhibited in a national group show called, "Looking for America," at the Washington Gallery of Photography in Bethesda, Maryland.

Baseball and Mitt,
Darien, Connecticut 2013

"Robert Carley is showing 'Flagman, Queens, NY,' a cibachrome of a flag-sporting citizen shot in the wake of 9/11 when Carley resolved to take pictures of nothing but American flags for a year. When the year was up, the idea still seemed fresh, so Carley has kept on taking flag pix (and has been able to get many of them into international art shows to boot)."

—Dan Bischoff, art critic for the Star-Ledger, Newark, NJ
quoted from a review of a show at the New Jersey Center for Visual Arts, 2/8/2004

The photo mentioned is on page 75.

Printed in the United States
by Baker & Taylor Publisher Services